MW01079062

weird but true!

SPACE

That's weird!

NASA IS WORKING ON A SPACE SUIT THAT COULD HEAL ITSELF IF TORN.

NATIONAL GEOGRAPHIC KiDS

weird but true!

SPACE

300
OUT-OF-THIS-WORLD FACTS

NATIONAL GEOGRAPHIC
WASHINGTON, D.C.

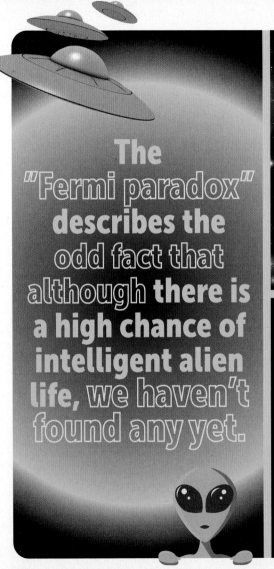

The "Fermi paradox" describes the odd fact that although **there is a high chance of intelligent alien life, we haven't found any yet.**

THE UNIVERSE IS ABOUT **13.8 BILLION** YEARS OLD. TO PUT THAT IN PERSPECTIVE, **13.8 BILLION SECONDS** EQUALS ABOUT **438 YEARS!**

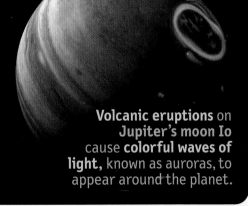

Volcanic eruptions on **Jupiter's moon Io** cause **colorful waves of light,** known as auroras, to appear around the planet.

Super-detailed photographs of the sun show giant pockets of boiling plasma, each about the size of the U.S. state of Texas.

PLASMA FLARE-UPS can eject ELECTRICALLY CHARGED superhot gases that CAUSE BLACKOUTS ON EARTH.

On average, the light from the entire universe combines to make a beige color that astronomers call **"cosmic latte."**

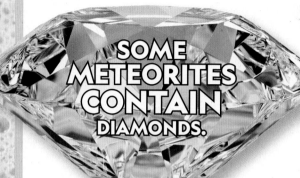

SOME METEORITES CONTAIN DIAMONDS.

In 2019, an astronomer discovered a "visiting" comet **made mostly of frozen poisonous gas** that traveled here from another solar system.

One **sports drink** company announced plans to **send** its drink powder **to the moon**—so a future astronaut can **drink it.**

MOONDUST—
A LAYER OF POWDERED MINERALS THAT COVERS THE MOON—IS TOXIC TO HUMANS.

Hello
my name is

The planet Uranus was once named

George.

When a secret government flying craft crashed in 1947 near Roswell, New Mexico, U.S.A., a government official tried to claim it was an alien spacecraft.

10

To this day, Roswell is home to a museum dedicated to UFOs.

One fast-food restaurant in Roswell is shaped like a UFO.

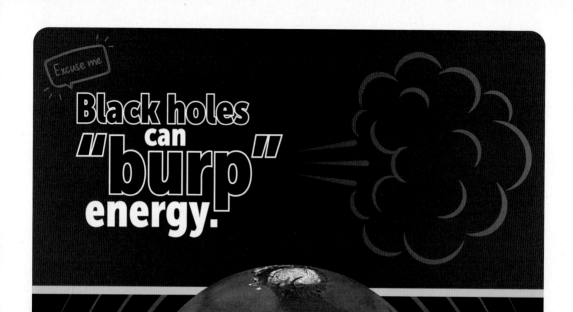

Excuse me

Black holes "can burp" energy.

MARS MAKES A CONSTANT HUMMING NOISE, BUT SCIENTISTS DON'T FULLY UNDERSTAND WHY.

SOME SCIENTISTS think it's possible that our **SOLAR SYSTEM** once had **TWO SUNS.**

Things on Earth that can be seen from space include ...

... giant blooms of tiny ocean organisms called phytoplankton.

... the Pyramids at Giza.

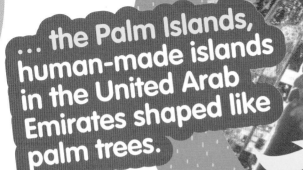

... the Palm Islands, human-made islands in the United Arab Emirates shaped like palm trees.

BEFORE

AFTER

... the Maha Kumbh Mela, a religious festival that takes place in northern India every 12 years.

15

A pizza was once delivered to the International Space Station (ISS) during a resupply mission.

Nothing to see here!

THE HOLLOW MOON THEORY IS THE IDEA THAT THE MOON IS ACTUALLY A HOLLOW SATELLITE CREATED BY ALIENS TO MONITOR EARTH.

(It's not.)

"Astronaut ice cream"—ice cream that has been freeze-dried—has never actually been taken to space.

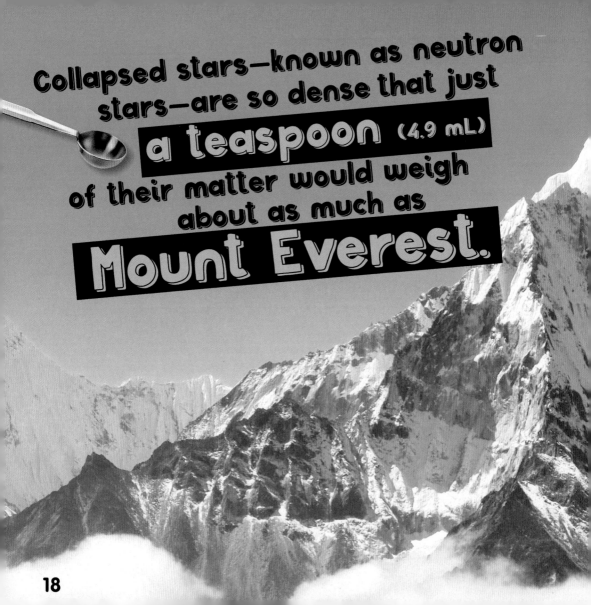

Collapsed stars—known as neutron stars—are so dense that just **a teaspoon** (4.9 mL) of their matter would weigh about as much as **Mount Everest.**

One tablespoon (15 mL) of **neutron star** material would **weigh more than 142 million** African elephants.

INCOMING!

ONE AREA OF THE PACIFIC OCEAN IS KNOWN AS THE SPACECRAFT CEMETERY BECAUSE IT HOLDS SO MANY RETIRED SATELLITES THAT WERE PROGRAMMED TO CRASH THERE.

R.I.P.

REST IN PIECES

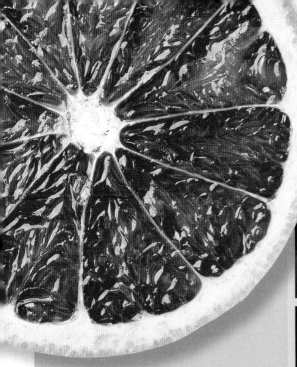

If the **sun** were the **size of a grapefruit,** then **Earth** would be the **size of the head of a pin.**

An ancient philosopher may have written one of the first references to aliens: He imagined people who lived on the moon and sweat milk.

A DOGHOUSE THAT WAS STRUCK BY A METEORITE WAS AUCTIONED FOR $44,100.

(THE DOG WAS UNHARMED.)

22

According to ancient Chinese legend, a goddess named Chang'e has lived on the moon ever since she was banished there for stealing a potion of immortality.

There is a **landing pad for UFOs** in Alberta, Canada.

FOR THOUSANDS OF YEARS, PEOPLE ACROSS EUROPE BELIEVED THAT THE FULL MOON COULD CAUSE MADNESS—SOMETIMES DUBBED "LUNACY" AFTER THE ROMAN WORD FOR "MOON."

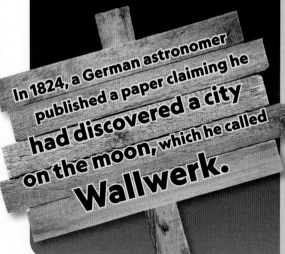

In 1824, a German astronomer published a paper claiming he had discovered a city on the moon, which he called **Wallwerk.**

One **SWIMSUIT COMPANY** designed some of its suits **USING NASA RESEARCH** in order to help people **SWIM FASTER.**

Ever since Yuri Gagarin, the first person to go to space, took a bathroom break near the tire of his transport bus, it has been tradition for Russian astronauts to pee on the bus's tire.

Scientists created a scent called "**space rose**" based on a rose that was sent on a space shuttle mission.

25

If you could drive STRAIGHT UP at 60 miles an hour (96.6 km/h), it would take only about AN HOUR TO GET TO SPACE.

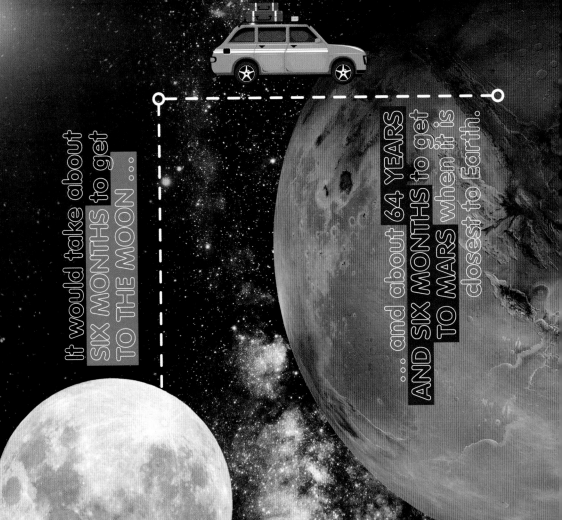

It would take about SIX MONTHS to get TO THE MOON ...

... and about 64 YEARS AND SIX MONTHS to get TO MARS when it is closest to Earth.

27

About
ONE MILLION EARTHS
could fit
INSIDE THE SUN.

A scientist discovered
what appears to be
a map of the moon
in a prehistoric
Irish tomb.

MOST SCORPIONS
GLOW BLUE
UNDER THE
LIGHT OF
A FULL MOON.

There are UFO-shaped hotels around the world.

Astronauts aboard the International Space Station once got "slimed" with **green goo** for a kids TV channel.

That's weird!

Scientists think it's possible for a moon to have its own moon—called a **moonmoon.**

(None have been discovered yet.)

One 17th-century English scientist proposed going to the moon in a chariot attached to a winglike sail.

NASA accidentally sold moondust collected by astronaut Neil Armstrong and tried (unsuccessfully) to get it back.

SOLD

31

The **GIANT CLOUDS** of gas and dust where many stars are created are known as **STAR NURSERIES.**

Across medieval Europe, many scientists believed that the sun and moon were planets.

During the Middle Ages, MANY EUROPEAN DOCTORS BELIEVED that a planet's location in the sky COULD HELP HEAL PEOPLE.

Because **wolves** usually howl at night, people once thought they were **howling at the moon.**

They're really howling to communicate with one another.

DARK ENERGY IS A MYSTERIOUS FORCE THAT SPEEDS UP THE RATE AT WHICH THE UNIVERSE IS EXPANDING.

In the 1960s,
a Finnish
architect
designed a
series of houses
shaped
like UFOs—
and many
remain,
abandoned
around
the world.

37

EARTH HAS MORE TREES THAN THE MILKY WAY HAS STARS.

The first structure built for studying the sky may be the Nabta Playa, a stone circle built in Egypt about 7,000 years ago.

Engineers are building a

GIANT HARPOON TO GET RID OF SPACE JUNK.

SPACE JUNK =
old spacecraft parts
that remain in orbit
around Earth

One stained-glass window at the National Cathedral in Washington, D.C., holds a piece of **moon rock.**

NASA's Hubble Space Telescope WEIGHS SOME **27,000 pounds** (12,250 kg) and is about the SIZE OF A **school bus.**

SCHOOL BUS

Scientists discovered an asteroid **shaped like a dog bone.**

Bow-WOW!

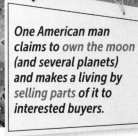

One American man claims to *own the moon* (and several planets) and makes a living by *selling parts* of it to interested buyers.

SCIENTISTS THINK THE MOON MAY HAVE FORMED FROM AN ANCIENT COLLISION ...

...BETWEEN EARTH AND ANOTHER PLANET.

WHOA!

43

The universe is about **27 percent dark matter**— matter that is not visible to us— but scientists still don't understand exactly what dark matter is made of.

To **protect** astronauts from radiation, **some spacecraft** may recycle **astronauts' poop** into space shields.

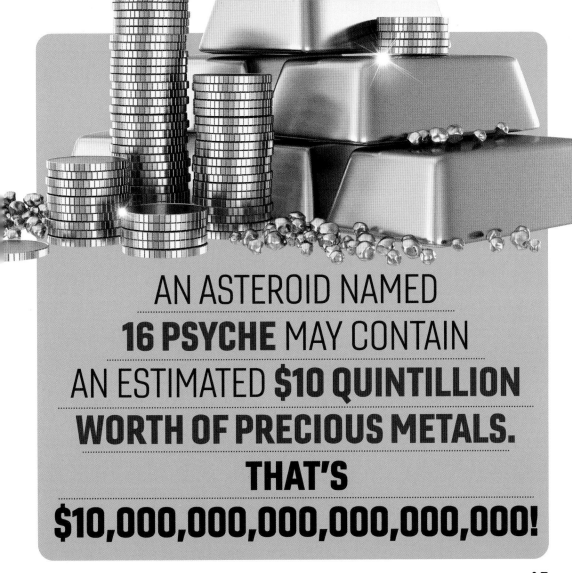

AN ASTEROID NAMED **16 PSYCHE** MAY CONTAIN AN ESTIMATED **$10 QUINTILLION WORTH OF PRECIOUS METALS.** **THAT'S** **$10,000,000,000,000,000,000!**

BLACK HOLES CAN SOMETIMES BRING "DEAD" STARS BRIEFLY BACK TO LIFE.

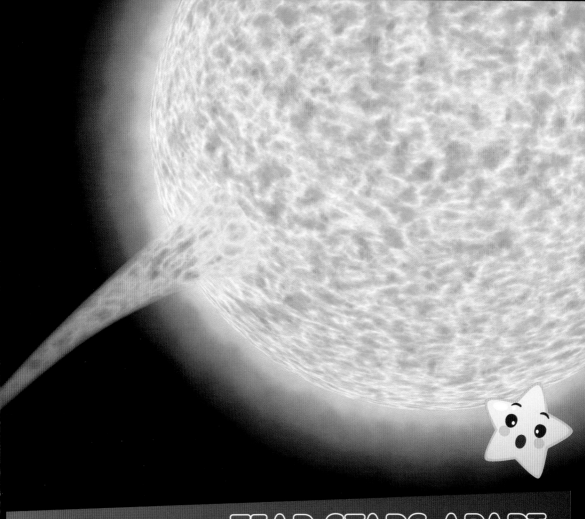

THEY CAN ALSO TEAR STARS APART.

One proposed NASA program would involve turning existing asteroids into **controlled spacecraft.**

EVEN TRAVELING AT THE SPEED OF LIGHT, IT WOULD TAKE ABOUT 200,000 YEARS TO CROSS THE MILKY WAY.

Jupiter is **SO MASSIVE** that every other planet could fit inside it **TWICE.**

Because **black holes** distort time, some scientists think they **could potentially** be used to **travel to the future.**

All aboard!
Next stop ...
tomorrow!

Some scientists believe there might be **white holes** — places in space that emit matter and cannot be entered by anything.

The magnetosphere—
a giant magnetic
field surrounding Earth—
protects us
from intense
SOLAR
STORMS.

IT TOOK
36 YEARS
FROM LAUNCH
FOR THE FIRST EVER
HUMAN-MADE OBJECT
TO TRAVEL OUT OF
OUR SOLAR SYSTEM.

Meteors in the annual Perseid shower contain many of the same ingredients found in breakfast cereal.

NASA
HAS PLANS TO
BUILD A
MOON
BASE CAMP.

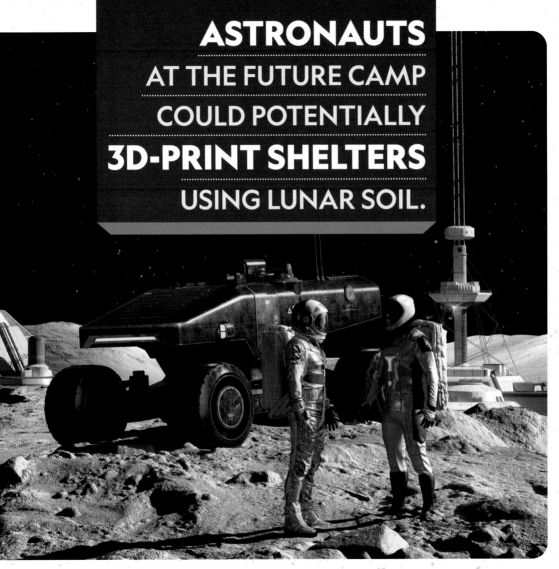

ASTRONAUTS
AT THE FUTURE CAMP
COULD POTENTIALLY
3D-PRINT SHELTERS
USING LUNAR SOIL.

Astronauts aboard the International Space Station came across a brand-new species of bacteria on their dining table.

The bacteria are not only harmless but actually may help humans better grow food in space.

A **ring of fire eclipse** is when the **moon** blocks out part of **the sun.**

A **total lunar eclipse**— when the **moon is in Earth's shadow**—is also called **a blood moon.**

57

The length of a day—the time it takes for a planet to rotate on its axis—is different for each planet. One day takes ...

... **11 hours** on Saturn.

... **10 hours** on Jupiter.

... **17 hours**
on Uranus.

... **1,408 hours**
on Mercury.

... **5,832 hours**
on Venus.

... **16 hours**
on Neptune.

... **25 hours**
on Mars.

An incredibly advanced telescope in Chile that can see into deep space is officially called the **VERY LARGE TELESCOPE.**

THE FIRST EVER RECORD OF A SOLAR ECLIPSE WAS CARVED INTO

STONES

IN IRELAND MORE THAN 5,000 YEARS AGO.

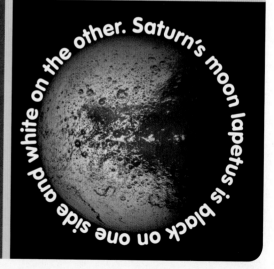

Saturn's moon Iapetus is black on one side and white on the other.

Experts are designing robotic snakes to explore the tunnels on Mars.

ASTEROIDS CAN VANISH INTO BLIND SPOTS NEAR THE SUN, MAKING IT IMPOSSIBLE FOR ASTRONOMERS TO DETECT THEM.

Astronauts wear a **white space suit** during space walks and an **easy-to-spot orange suit** during takeoffs and landings.

Scientists may have discovered **19 NEW** EXOPLANETS by detecting traces of auroras— the same phenomena that cause **EARTH'S** northern lights.

The asteroid that helped wipe out most dinosaurs was likely some six miles (10 km) long—about the length of Paris.

DURING THE UFO FESTIVAL IN McMINNVILLE, OREGON, U.S.A.,

That's weird!

PARTICIPANTS—AND THEIR PETS—DRESS LIKE ALIENS.

65

Moon milk is the name of a traditional healing drink known for helping people sleep.

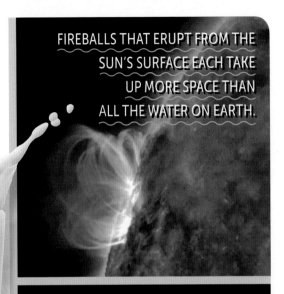

FIREBALLS THAT ERUPT FROM THE SUN'S SURFACE EACH TAKE UP MORE SPACE THAN ALL THE WATER ON EARTH.

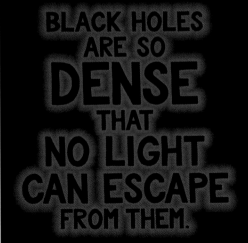

BLACK HOLES ARE SO **DENSE** THAT NO LIGHT CAN ESCAPE FROM THEM.

One **RESTAURANT** at Walt Disney World is **DESIGNED TO MAKE IT SEEM** as if diners are **EATING ON A SPACE STATION** above Earth.

When galaxies **collide,**

one can **"eat"** the other.

People known as **eclipse hunters** travel the world to **experience as many solar eclipses as possible.**

One way to fight climate change could be to create giant chemical bubbles in space to shield the planet from solar radiation.

69

A star-forming cloud that looks like it is chomping through space is nicknamed the Pac-Man nebula.

Ahhhh!

DURING SPRINGTIME ON MARS, A THIN LAYER OF ICE ON THE PLANET'S SURFACE MELTS, CREATING A HONEYCOMB PATTERN.

Saturn's bands change color as seasons change on the planet.

71

AN ALIEN MONSTER IN *STAR WARS* WAS INSPIRED BY THE ANT LION, AN INSECT THAT HIDES IN A PIT IN THE SAND AND LUNGES OUT TO GRAB PREY.

Giant "clouds"
of water in space
contain 140 trillion times
more water than all
the oceans and lakes on Earth.

SCIENTISTS DISCOVERED A PLANET WHERE IT POSSIBLY— RAINS GLASS— SIDEWAYS.

A ROGUE PLANET IS A PLANET-SIZE OBJECT THAT DOESN'T ORBIT A STAR— SOME OF THEM MAY HAVE ESCAPED THEIR STAR'S GRAVITY.

One exoplanet has GIANT RINGS about 200 TIMES THE SIZE of those around Saturn.

There are litter boxes that make it look as if your cat is piloting a UFO.

The center of Earth is as hot as the surface of the sun.

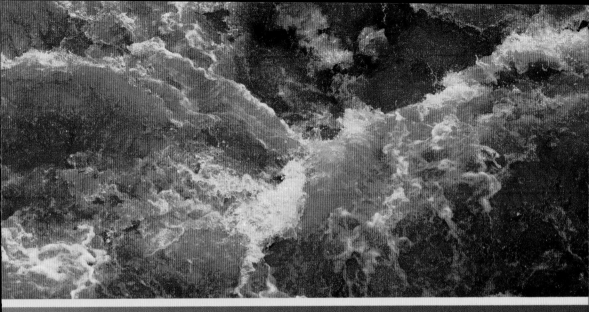

Sunsets on Mars are BLUE.

That's weird!

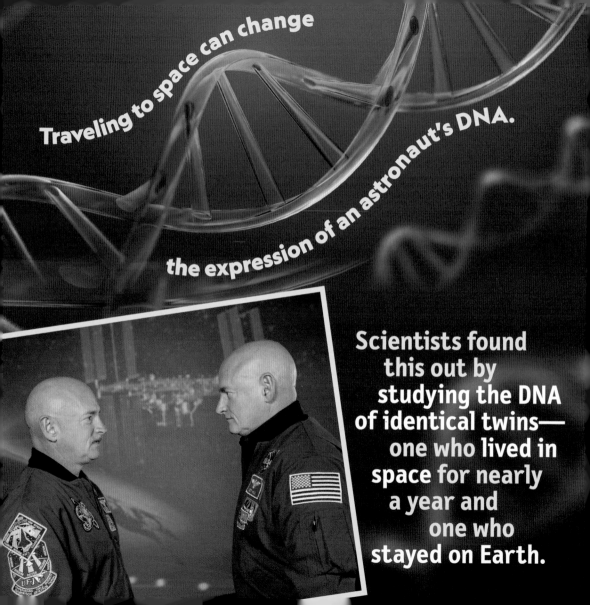

Traveling to space can change the expression of an astronaut's DNA.

Scientists found this out by studying the DNA of identical twins— one who lived in space for nearly a year and one who stayed on Earth.

Scientists can figure out
what stars are made of
just by looking at the
COLORS OF LIGHT
they emit.

A DEAD GALAXY
IS ONE THAT HAS RUN OUT OF THE COLD
HYDROGEN GASES IT NEEDS TO MAKE STARS.

IN SPACE, **DEAD SKIN** (LIKE THE CALLOUSES ON FEET) FALLS OFF ALL AT ONCE AND IN CHUNKS!

ARCHAEOLOGISTS HAVE USED **SPACE SATELLITES** TO REDISCOVER **ANCIENT MAYA CITIES** IN GUATEMALA.

Some experts think that, over time, **living on Mars could cause humans to evolve** into a new species.

FARAWAY STARS THAT ARE
MOVING AWAY
FROM EARTH
APPEAR RED.

STARS
**MOVING
CLOSER**
TO EARTH
LOOK BLUE.

An 18th-century botanist in Britain came up with several new constellations, including a slug, a worm, and a toad—but none of them caught on.

TO EXPLORE RUGGED GROUND, NASA DEVELOPED AN INSECTLIKE ROBOT WITH SIX LEGS.

83

Eruptions on Jupiter's moon Io can send volcanic gases more than

300 MILES (500 KM) into space.

According to previously **classified documents,** former British prime minister **Winston Churchill** may have worked to **cover up** a supposed **UFO sighting.**

How's my hair?

Winds on Neptune can be faster than the speed of sound.

People in ancient China sometimes used "moonmilk"—a mineral ooze found in caves—as face cream.

(No relation to the drink on page 66!)

BECAUSE TINY GRAINS COULD DAMAGE EQUIPMENT, ASTRONAUTS ARE NOT ALLOWED TO USE SALT SHAKERS IN SPACE.

Neptune seems to be slowly cooling—and scientists don't know why.

Most astronaut **poop** is loaded into a cargo vessel that **burns up in the atmosphere** ... but **some is brought back to Earth** to be studied.

ONE EXOPLANET IS MAGENTA

THE ENTIRE EARTH IS COVERED IN COSMIC DUST—THE TINY BITS OF MATTER THAT MAKE UP THE UNIVERSE.

Scientists are considering adding **microphones to astronauts' boots,** as being able to better **hear their own footsteps** may help them **avoid tripping.**

ONE **SOLAR SYSTEM** IS HOME TO **SEVEN EARTHLIKE PLANETS**—MEANING PLANETS THAT **COULD POTENTIALLY SUPPORT LIFE.**

A study found that the phases of the moon can affect people's sleep.

ZZZZ

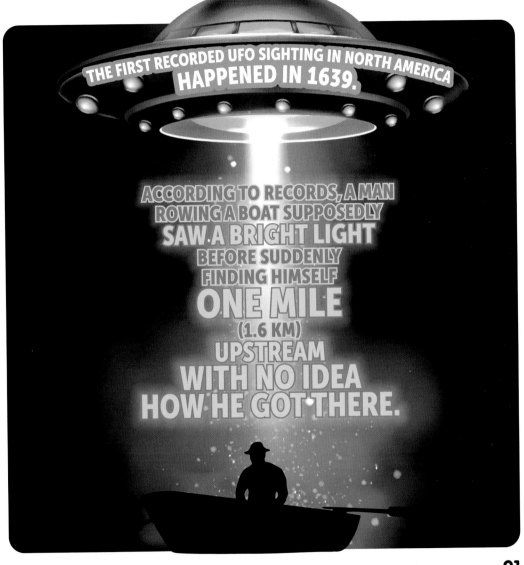

THE FIRST RECORDED UFO SIGHTING IN NORTH AMERICA HAPPENED IN 1639.

ACCORDING TO RECORDS, A MAN ROWING A BOAT SUPPOSEDLY SAW A BRIGHT LIGHT BEFORE SUDDENLY FINDING HIMSELF ONE MILE (1.6 KM) UPSTREAM WITH NO IDEA HOW HE GOT THERE.

Ancient Romans believed that a gem called moonstone was made from solidified moonbeams.

SCIENTISTS ARE DEVELOPING A LETTUCE THAT COULD HELP STRENGTHEN ASTRONAUTS' BONES WHILE THEY ARE IN SPACE.

Scientists launched *worms into space* to study *how astronauts lose muscle mass* in microgravity.

Boo!

NASA turned electromagnetic waves measured on Jupiter's moon Ganymede into audio. (They sounded like spooky howls and whistles.)

93

Glowing gases around the **supermassive black hole** at the center of the Milky Way form a **doughnut shape.**

Scientists are developing a submarine to explore Kraken Mare, a roughly 1,000-foot (305-m)-deep lake on Titan, Saturn's largest moon.

MORE THAN 100 GEYSERS GUSH WATER AND TINY GRAINS OF ICE NEAR THE SOUTH POLE OF SATURN'S MOON ENCELADUS.

THESE GEYSER ERUPTIONS HELP ADD TO ONE OF THE PLANET'S RINGS, WHICH SPANS MORE THAN 600,000 MILES (966,000 KM).

A NASA ROBOT NAMED **ICE WORM** MAY ONE DAY **CLIMB UP** THE **FROZEN TERRAIN** OF **ICY PLANETS.**

New stars will be born from the hot gases that form the glowing "eyes" of the Ghost Head Nebula.

MARINER VALLEY ON MARS could stretch across the continental UNITED STATES.

ONE EXOPLANET MAY BE HOME TO A **TYPE OF "ICE"** THAT REACHES TEMPERATURES OF NEARLY 1000°F (540°C) **BUT NEVER MELTS.**

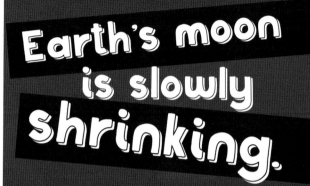

Earth's moon is slowly shrinking.

The strongest substance in the universe is called **nuclear pasta;** it's the noodle-like leftovers of a dead star.

The length of a year—the time it takes for a planet to orbit the sun—is different for each planet. In Earth days, one year takes...

... 225 DAYS
ON VENUS.

... 687 DAYS
ON MARS.

... 88 DAYS
ON MERCURY.

... 4,333 DAYS
ON JUPITER.

... **10,756 DAYS**
ON SATURN.

... **60,190 DAYS**
ON NEPTUNE.

... **30,687 DAYS**
ON URANUS.

Yummm!

On the International Space Station, astronauts drink their recycled sweat and urine.

To keep floating breadcrumbs from damaging instruments on a spacecraft, astronauts eat **peanut butter and jelly on tortillas** instead of bread.

SCIENTISTS THINK THE ASTEROID THAT LED TO THE EXTINCTION OF MOST DINOSAURS STRUCK IN THE SPRING.

SCIENTISTS ARE DEVELOPING THREADLIKE SPACE PROBES THAT MIMIC HOW A CRAB SPIDER SHOOTS SILK STRANDS TO TRAVEL THROUGH THE AIR.

A single M&M candy carried on board SpaceShipOne, the first privately crewed vehicle to reach space, sold for $1,400.

Saturn's moon Mimas has been compared to the Death Star because its shape resembles the *Star Wars* spacecraft.

THERE ARE FLAT, PANCAKE-SHAPED VOLCANOES ON VENUS.

Chocolate chip cookies were the **first food to** be baked in space.

Planets that orbit two suns are called
TATOOINE PLANETS
after Luke Skywalker's home planet
IN *STAR WARS.*

"Jingle Bells" was the first song played in space.

THE MOON LOOKS ROUND FROM EARTH, BUT IT IS ACTUALLY EGG-SHAPED.

SCIENTISTS CAN FIGURE OUT WHERE PENGUINS LIVE BY SPOTTING THEIR POOP FROM SPACE.

SOME OF THE VOLCANIC GAS FOUND ON IO, ONE OF JUPITER'S MOONS, GLOWS IN THE DARK.

Astronauts have brought back **842 POUNDS** (382 kg) of rocks and soil **from the moon.**

ONE GALAXY'S GRAVITATIONAL FORCES ARE SO STRONG, THEY'RE **PULLING APART** A LARGER GALAXY THAT'S TENS OF THOUSANDS OF LIGHT-YEARS AWAY.

As an astronaut was floating in space, the wedding ring he'd lost in his spacecraft floated out of the hatch and hit the back of his helmet.

ABOUT
22,000 POUNDS
(10,000 KG)
OF RAIN
FALLS FROM SATURN'S RINGS
EVERY SECOND.

EARTH'S MOON HAS LAVA TUBES, OR VOLCANIC TUNNELS, THAT ARE **SO BIG** THEY COULD FIT A SMALL CITY—SKYSCRAPERS INCLUDED.

114

A SATELLITE MAPPED THE LOCATION OF ALMOST **TWO BILLION** STARS IN THE MILKY WAY GALAXY— ONLY ABOUT **2 PERCENT** OF THE TOTAL.

Clouds on Uranus smell like rotten eggs.

EWWW!

ROBOTS THAT SEARCH FOR LIFE ON MARS "PRACTICED" IN SOUTH AMERICA'S ATACAMA DESERT, ONE OF THE **DRIEST PLACES** ON EARTH.

One pair of galaxies looks like a penguin guarding its egg.

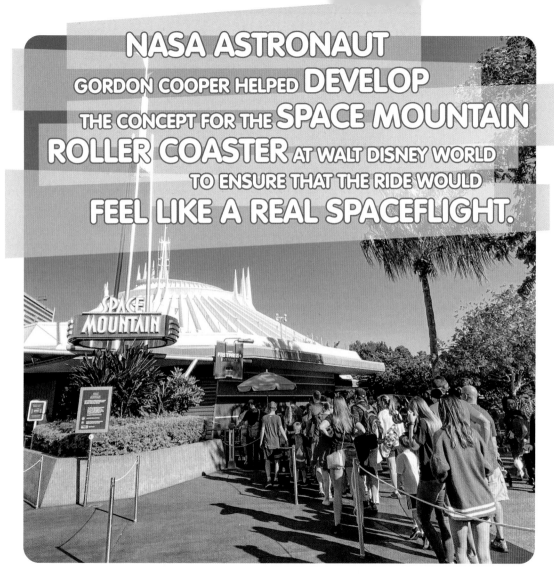

NASA ASTRONAUT GORDON COOPER HELPED **DEVELOP** THE CONCEPT FOR THE **SPACE MOUNTAIN** **ROLLER COASTER** AT WALT DISNEY WORLD TO ENSURE THAT THE RIDE WOULD **FEEL LIKE A REAL SPACEFLIGHT.**

A Grogu plush rode aboard a SpaceX launch so that when the toy began to float in near-zero gravity, the crew would know they'd reached **orbit.**

That's weird!

Meteors can glow **purple,** green, blue, orange, or yellow as they speed through the sky.

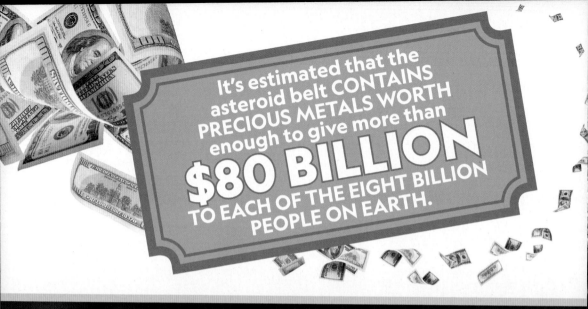

It's estimated that the asteroid belt CONTAINS PRECIOUS METALS WORTH enough to give more than **$80 BILLION** TO EACH OF THE EIGHT BILLION PEOPLE ON EARTH.

YOU CAN SEE A "SPACE JELLYFISH" WHEN THE SETTING SUN REFLECTS OFF A LAUNCHED ROCKET'S TRAIL OF GASES.

HUMAN URINE COULD BE USED TO CREATE "LUNAR CONCRETE" FOR BUILDING A SETTLEMENT ON THE MOON.

A piece of the **Wright brothers' first plane flew with the first helicopter** to touch down **on Mars.**

If we could hear the sun from Earth, it would sound about as loud as standing next to a speaker at a rock concert.

Astronauts train for **space walks underwater.**

125

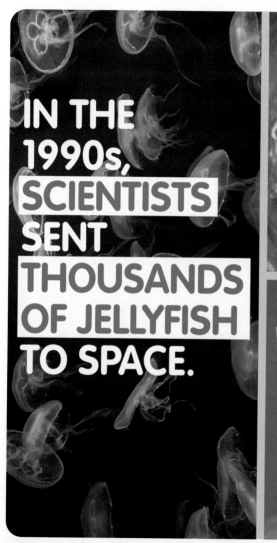

IN THE 1990s, SCIENTISTS SENT THOUSANDS OF JELLYFISH TO SPACE.

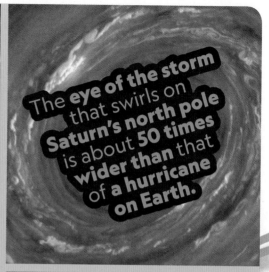

The **eye of the storm** that swirls on **Saturn's north pole** is about **50 times wider than** that of **a hurricane on Earth.**

In 1947, fruit flies became the first animals ever sent to space.

A TOILET ON THE INTERNATIONAL SPACE STATION COST **$23 MILLION.**

The toothbrush that Buzz Aldrin took on Apollo 11 sold for

$18,400 in 2004.

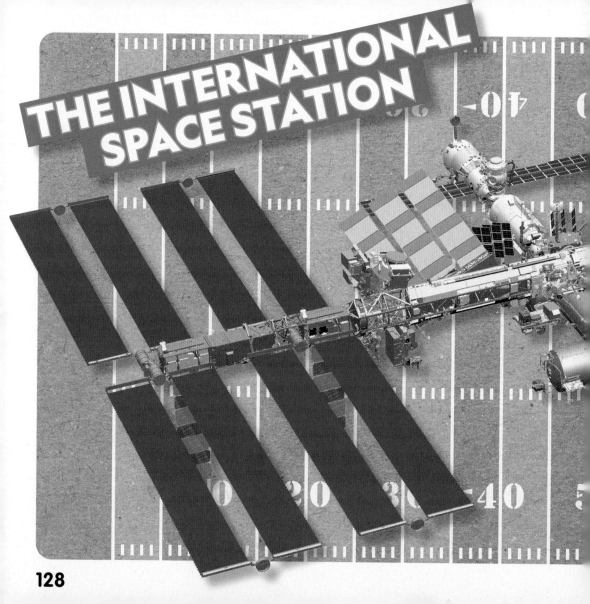

THE INTERNATIONAL SPACE STATION

IS ABOUT THE LENGTH OF AN AMERICAN FOOTBALL FIELD.

Kathryn Sullivan is the first person to both walk in space ...

... and visit Challenger Deep, the deepest part of the ocean.

130

During the live broadcast of the **Apollo 14 mission** in 1971, astronaut Alan Shepard hit **golf balls** on the moon.

(Two golf balls are still on the moon.)

MOONDUST IS SO SHARP THAT IT WORE THROUGH THREE LAYERS OF AN ASTRONAUT'S BOOT.

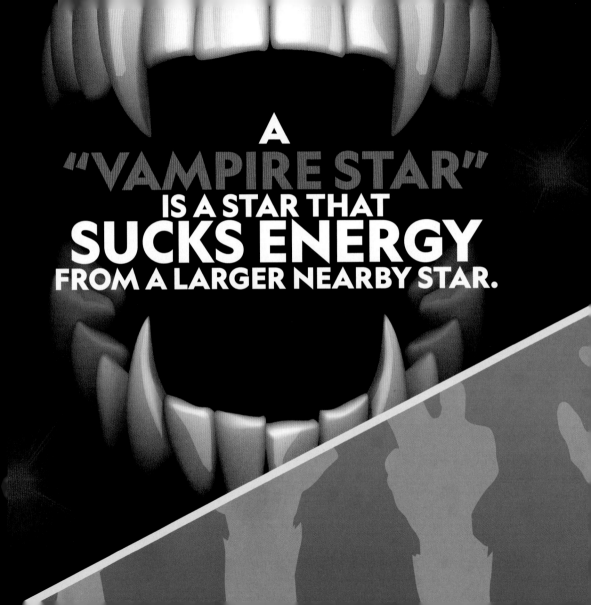

A "ZOMBIE STAR" IS A STAR THAT EXPLODED BUT DID NOT DIE.

ASTRONAUTS ON THE INTERNATIONAL SPACE STATION PLAYED WITH SLIME TO LEARN HOW IT REACTED TO THE LACK OF GRAVITY.

Two volcanoes almost as tall as Mount Everest once spewed icy lava on Pluto.

If the Hubble Space Telescope were in Los Angeles, it could focus in on the light of a firefly in Istanbul, Turkey.

135

The Hubble Space Telescope helped determine the age of the universe—**about 13.8 billion years.**

About **seven new stars are born** in the Milky Way galaxy **each year.**

SpaceX launched a Tesla Roadster car with a mannequin driver into orbit around the sun.

137

ASTRONOMERS HAVE TURNED THE DIGITAL DATA CAPTURED BY TELESCOPES INTO SOUND SO THAT WE CAN HEAR AN EXPLODING STAR.

THE TADPOLE GALAXY, NAMED FOR ITS "TAIL" OF STARS, GAS, AND DUST, WILL LIKELY LOSE ITS TAIL AS IT GROWS OLDER, JUST LIKE A REAL TADPOLE.

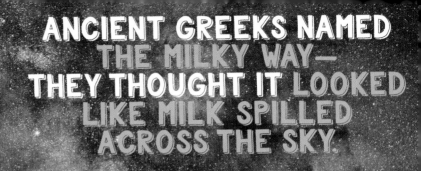

ANCIENT GREEKS NAMED THE MILKY WAY— THEY THOUGHT IT LOOKED LIKE MILK SPILLED ACROSS THE SKY.

WITHOUT GRAVITY, ASTRONAUTS CAN'T LIE DOWN TO SLEEP— SO THEY STRAP THEIR SLEEPING BAGS TO WALLS.

Toy Story's **Buzz Lightyear** was named for astronaut **Buzz Aldrin,** one of the first two people to walk on the moon.

Charlie Brown and Snoopy were mascots of the Apollo 10 mission.

TETRIS WAS THE FIRST VIDEO GAME PLAYED IN SPACE.

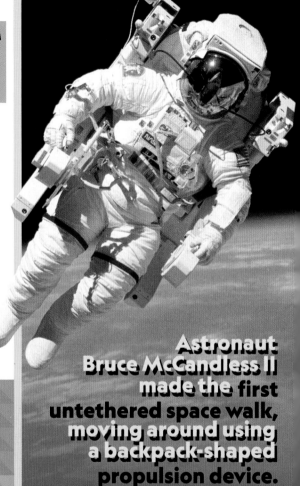

Astronaut Bruce McCandless II made the first untethered space walk, moving around using a backpack-shaped propulsion device.

143

NASA'S JUNO SPACECRAFT CAPTURED GREEN LIGHTNING STRIKING JUPITER'S NORTH POLE.

An astronaut's **space suit** for a space shuttle flight weighs about

300 pounds
(136 kg)
on Earth—
about
as much as a
refrigerator.

THERE IS AN ENORMOUS "HOLE" IN THE MILKY WAY THAT MAY HAVE BEEN CAUSED BY A GIANT SUPERNOVA MILLIONS OF YEARS AGO.

SOME SCIENTISTS IN CHINA THINK THAT **PLANTS GROWN IN SPACE** MAY PRODUCE SEEDS THAT **COULD HELP GROW MORE FOOD ON EARTH.**

Scientists have observed that two **"MOONS"** made of giant clouds of space dust may be **ORBITING EARTH.**

Hundreds of spinning **dust tornadoes on Mars** created a pattern that looked like a hairy spider.

146

ASTRONAUTS HAVE PLAYED MUSICAL INSTRUMENTS IN SPACE.

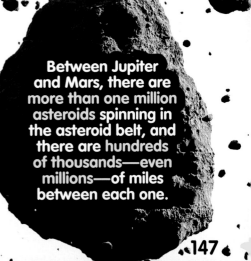

Between Jupiter and Mars, there are more than one million asteroids spinning in the asteroid belt, and there are hundreds of thousands—even millions—of miles between each one.

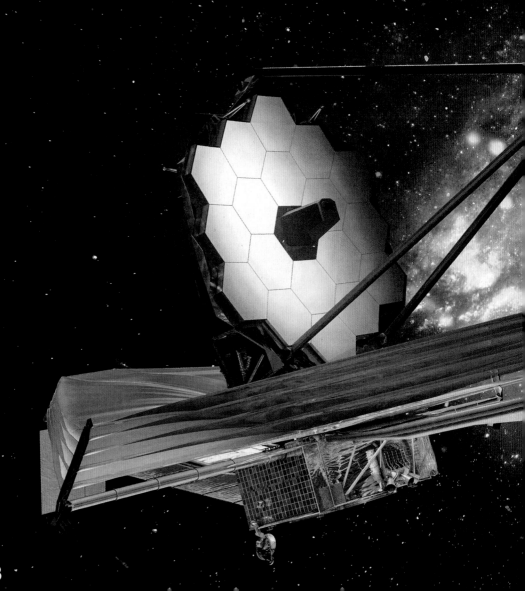

THE JAMES WEBB SPACE TELESCOPE IS KEPT COOL BY A SUNSHIELD THE SIZE OF A TENNIS COURT.

THE **MOON MOVES** ABOUT 1.5 INCHES (3.8 CM) **AWAY FROM EARTH** EACH YEAR.

Astronauts'
eyeballs
change shape
after spending time
in space.

HAUMEA'S **SUPERFAST ROTATION** SPINS THE DWARF PLANET **INTO THE SHAPE OF** AN AMERICAN FOOTBALL.

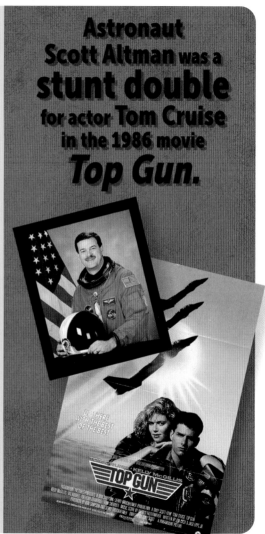

Astronaut Scott Altman was a **stunt double** for actor **Tom Cruise** in the 1986 movie *Top Gun.*

151

152

MARS HAS SNOWSTORMS.

A **SOLAR ECLIPSE** ENDED A SIX-YEAR WAR IN 585 B.C.: SOLDIERS READ THE **SUDDENLY DARKENED SKY** AS A SIGN TO STOP FIGHTING.

TWO ROCKET SCIENTISTS CREATED **ASTRO POP** LOLLIPOPS IN 1963, MODELING THE CANDY AFTER **A ROCKET.**

NASA created a playlist of eerie space sounds for Halloween.

Spooky!

155

The explosion of a star that was 20 times the mass of our sun created the Veil Nebula.

ASTRONAUTS ABOARD THE TROUBLED APOLLO 13 MISSION USED **DUCT TAPE,** **TUBE SOCKS,** AND **OTHER MATERIALS** TO MODIFY AN AIR FILTER— ALLOWING THEM TO **RETURN** **HOME SAFELY.**

Astronaut John Young **smuggled a corned beef sandwich into his flight** suit for the Gemini 3 mission in 1965.

The remains of an ancient planet that once collided with Earth might still be buried beneath Earth's surface.

157

Eight miles (13 km) of wire bring power to the electrical systems on the International Space Station—that's longer than the perimeter of New York City's **Central Park.**

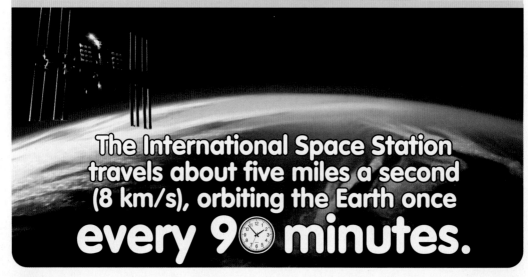

The International Space Station travels about five miles a second (8 km/s), orbiting the Earth once **every 90 minutes.**

TO ESCAPE EARTH'S GRAVITY, A ROCKET TRAVELS ABOUT **30 TIMES FASTER** THAN A COMMERCIAL AIRPLANE.

161

Neptune is the only planet in our solar system that can't be seen from Earth with the naked eye.

THE SOLAR SYSTEM'S **BIGGEST VOLCANO,** OLYMPUS MONS ON MARS, IS ABOUT **THREE TIMES THE HEIGHT OF MOUNT EVEREST,** EARTH'S TALLEST MOUNTAIN.

THE WORD "ASTRONAUT" COMES FROM GREEK WORDS MEANING "STAR SAILOR."

Earth has "quasi-moons": asteroids that follow the planet as it orbits the sun.

THE PARTICLES OF  **ICE** AND 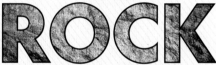 **ROCK** THAT FORM **SATURN'S RINGS** CAN BE AS SMALL AS A GRAIN OF SAND OR AS LARGE AS A MOUNTAIN.

Astronauts can **grow** up to **3 percent taller** during long stays in space.

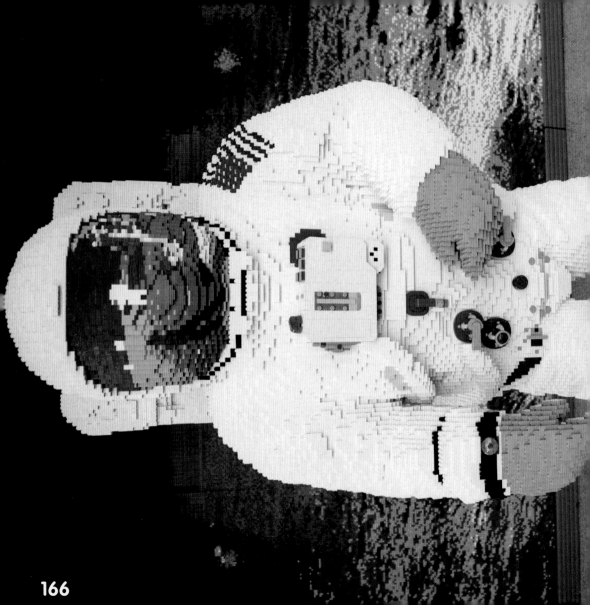

To celebrate the 50th anniversary of the Apollo 11 launch, Lego built a life-size astronaut model made with

30,000 Lego bricks.

The Sea of Tranquility on **Earth's moon** is not made of water; it's a **plain of hardened lava.**

Wheee!

The fastest known star orbits the supermassive black hole in the Milky Way's center, moving at about 5,000 miles a second (8,000 km/s).

The Milky Way galaxy and the Andromeda galaxy

will collide in about 4.5 billion years.

Astronaut Karen Nyberg created a collection of fabrics based on photos she took of Earth from the International Space Station.

France

Balls of heat and light about the size of France zip across the sun at 125,000 miles an hour (201,000 km/h).

EUROPE

O-stars, the most massive kind of star known, created a ring of glowing infrared dust in the Milky Way, invisible to the human eye.

On Neptune and Uranus, it can rain diamonds.

An 11-year-old girl gave **Pluto** its name in 1930.

VENUS AND URANUS SPIN BACKWARD.

That's weird!

"Blue blobs" are **star systems** with tons of **blue stars**, the **hottest** kind of star.

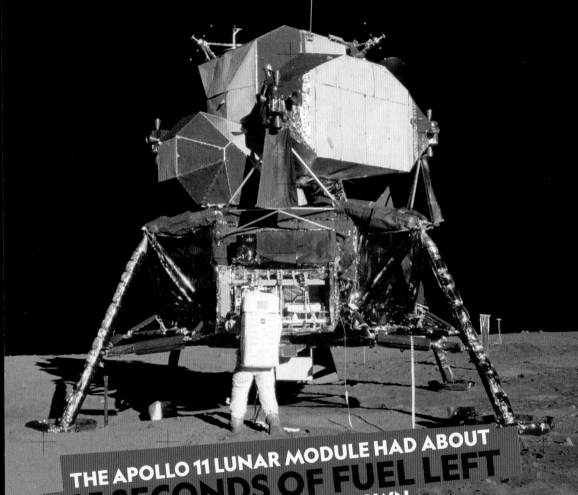

THE APOLLO 11 LUNAR MODULE HAD ABOUT **45 SECONDS OF FUEL LEFT** WHEN IT TOUCHED DOWN FOR THE FIRST MOON LANDING.

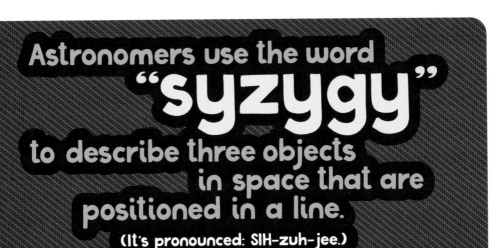

Astronomers use the word **"syzygy"** to describe three objects in space that are positioned in a line.

(It's pronounced: SIH-zuh-jee.)

Sausage stars are named for the shape of their orbital path.

MORE THAN **200 ROCKS** FROM MARS HAVE FALLEN TO EARTH.

Anyone else getting dizzy?

When fish and tadpoles were taken to space, they swam in circles instead of straight.

That's cool!

THE CLOUDS ABOVE SATURN'S NORTH POLE SWIRL IN A HEXAGON SHAPE.

MERCURY SPINS SO SLOWLY THAT IT TAKES LONGER TO COMPLETE ONE SOLAR DAY THAN TO ORBIT THE SUN, MAKING A DAY ON THE PLANET LONGER THAN ITS YEAR.

In 1859, the biggest solar storm on record caused sparks to shower from telegraph machines across the world.

The storm also caused the northern lights, normally seen closer to the Arctic Circle, to be spotted from the beaches of Hawaii, U.S.A.

That's weird!

179

CONSTELLATIONS SEEN FROM THE **SOUTHERN HEMISPHERE** APPEAR **UPSIDE DOWN** WHEN VIEWED FROM THE **NORTHERN HEMISPHERE.**

The Milky Way is sandwiched **between two** giant bubbles of gas.

The LONGEST space walk lasted **8 hours 56 minutes.**

Only about **5 percent** of the universe can be **seen** with a telescope.

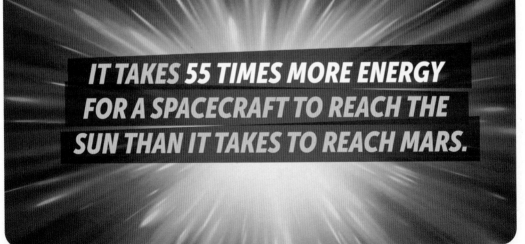

IT TAKES 55 TIMES MORE ENERGY FOR A SPACECRAFT TO REACH THE SUN THAN IT TAKES TO REACH MARS.

During some of its orbits around the sun, NASA's Parker Solar Probe traveled fast enough to go from New York City to Tokyo in less than a minute.

183

A STACK OF **DIRTY DISHES** HELPED INSPIRE THE SHAPE OF THE *MILLENNIUM FALCON* FROM *STAR WARS.*

185

ABOUT ONE MILLION PEOPLE SENT THEIR NAMES TO BE INCLUDED ON A MEMORY CARD TRAVELING WITH THE PARKER SOLAR PROBE TO THE SUN.

THE METEORS THAT WE SEE IN THE PERSEID SHOWER COME FROM A COMET THAT IS ALMOST TWICE THE SIZE OF THE ASTEROID THAT WIPED OUT THE DINOSAURS.

Scientists think that **Jupiter** became the **largest planet** in our solar system by "eating" other planets.

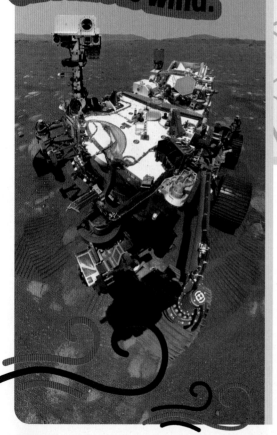

The only natural sound that the Perseverance rover has picked up **on Mars** is wind.

AT THE **NATIONAL AIR AND SPACE MUSEUM** IN WASHINGTON, D.C., YOU CAN **TOUCH A ROCK** FROM THE **MOON.**

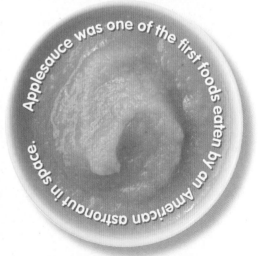

Applesauce was one of the first foods eaten by an American astronaut in space.

188

THERE IS A LOT OF JUNK IN SPACE—AT LEAST 23,000 HUMAN-MADE OBJECTS ORBIT EARTH.

Talk about a waste of space ...

189

The Gaia spacecraft captured images of fiery tsunamis moving across several stars in the Milky Way.

Scientists have developed a way to turn astronauts' poop into food for lengthy space missions.

That's weird!

YOU CAN **SPEND THE NIGHT** IN A MODEL OF THE **APOLLO 11 SPACECRAFT.**

UNITED STATES

INTEGRATED TEST STAND Nº 1

"Moon trees" grow in the United States, sprouted from hundreds of seeds that were launched into space.

NASA SCIENTISTS DISCOVERED A TEARDROP-SHAPED STAR THAT BRIGHTENS AND DIMS ON ONLY ONE SIDE.

Some astronauts attach Velcro inside their space suit helmets to scratch itches.

NASA'S STARDUST CAPSULE USED A TENNIS-RACKET-LIKE DEVICE TO CAPTURE COMET PARTICLES AND BRING THEM BACK TO EARTH.

Earth is in what scientists call the **Goldilocks Zone—** it's the "just-right" distance from the sun to support life.

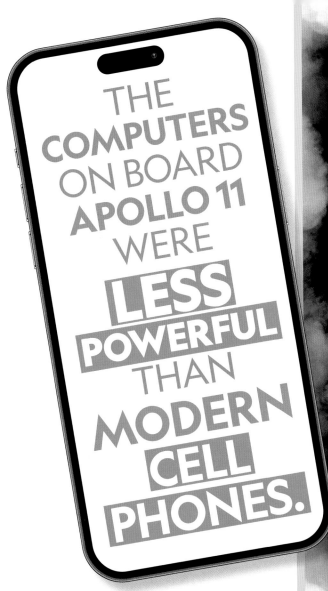

THE **COMPUTERS** ON BOARD **APOLLO 11** WERE **LESS POWERFUL** THAN **MODERN CELL PHONES.**

NASA developed a **fragrance** to help **astronauts in training** get used to **the smoky scent of space.**

A town in Germany was built with **15-million-year-old diamond dust** produced from an enormous asteroid striking Earth.

The town sits on the asteroid's crater, and it's estimated that the crater contains more than **72,000 tons** (65,000 t) of the gemstone.

An astronaut's **space suit** protects against **extreme temperatures** in space, from minus **250°F** (-157°C)

to **250°F** (121°C).

FACTFINDER

Boldface indicates illustrations.

A

Alberta, Canada 24, **24**
Aldrin, Buzz 127, **127**, 140
Alien life
  ancient references to 21
  Fermi paradox 4, **4**
  hollow moon theory 16, **16**
  potential for 90, **90**, 194, **194**
  search for 117, **117**
  spacecraft 10–11, **10–11**
  see also UFOs
Altman, Scott 151, **151**
Ancient astronomy 38, **38**, 60,
  139, **139**
Andromeda galaxy 169, **169**
Ant lions 72, **72**
Apollo 10 142, **142**
Apollo 11 127, **166–167**, 167, 174,
  174, 191, **191**, 195
Apollo 13 156, **156**
Apollo 14 131, **131**
Applesauce 188, **188**
Archaeology 80, **80**
Armstrong, Neil 31
Asteroids
  in asteroid belt 147, **147**
  craters 196
  diamond dust from 196
  dinosaur extinction 63, **63**,
    103, **103**, 186, **186**
  precious metals in 45, 122
  "quasi-moons" 164, **164**
  shaped like dog bone 41
  turned into spacecraft 48, **48**
  vanishing in blind spots 61, **61**
Astro Pop lollipops 154, **154**
Astronaut ice cream 17, **17**
Astronauts
  Apollo 13 156
  boots 89, **89**, 131, **131**
  dead skin 80
  DNA changes 78, **78**
  eyeballs changing shape 150
  firsts 130, **130**
  growth while in space 165
  helmets 193, **193**
  identical twins 78, **78**
  ISS bacteria 56, **56**
  Lego **166–167**, 167
  loss of muscle mass 93
  moon base camp 54–55,
    54–55
  moondust collected by 31, **31**
  musical instruments 147, **147**
  peeing on bus tire 25
  poop 44, 88, **88**, 190, **190**
  radiation protection 44
  roller coasters 119, **119**
  scratching itches 193, **193**
  sleeping 139, **139**
  slime and 30, 134, **134**
  space suits 3, **3**, 62, **62**, 144,
    198–199, **198–199**
  space walks 62, **62**, 181, **181**
  as stunt double 151, **151**
  toothbrush sales price 127
  training 125, **125**, 195
  tripping prevention 89, **89**
  wedding ring 113, **113**
  word origin 164
  World Series pitch 160
  see also Food in space
Auroras 4, **4**, 62, **62**

B

Bacteria 56, **56**
Baseball 160, **160**
Black holes 12, **12**, 46–47, **46–47**,
  50–51, **50–51**, 66, 94, 168, **168**
Blood moon 57, **57**
"Blue blobs" 173, **173**
Bowersox, Kenneth 160
Buzz Lightyear 140, **141**

C

Cats 75, **75**
Challenger Deep 130, **130**
Charlie Brown 142, **142**
Chinese legends 23, **23**

Chocolate chip cookies 107, **107**
Churchill, Winston 85
Climate change 69
Clouds 72, **72**, 116, **116**, 177, **177**
Collapsed stars 18–19
Columbia (space shuttle) 160
Comets 8, **8**, 186, **186**, 193
Constellations 82, **82**, 180, **180**, 197
Cooper, Gordon 119
Cosmic dust 89, **89**
Cosmic latte 8, **8**
Crab spiders 104, **104**
Cruise, Tom 151, **151**

D

Dark energy 35
Dark matter 44
Day length 58–59, **58–59**
Dead stars 46, **46**, 99
Diamonds 8, **8**, 172, **172**, 196
Dinosaur extinction 63, **63**, 103, **103**, 186, **186**
DNA 78, **78**
Doghouse 22, **22**

E

Earth
ancient collisions 42–43, **42–43**, 157, **157**
cosmic dust 89, **89**
heat at center 76, **76–77**
northern lights 62, **62**
"quasi-moons" 164, **164**
radiation shields 69
seen from space 14–15, **14–15**
size 21, 28, **28**
trees 38, **38**
Eclipses 57, **57**, 60, 69, **69**, 154
Egypt 14, **14**, 38, **38**
Enceladus (Saturn's moon) 95, **95**
Evolution 80, **80**
Exomoon 21, **21**
Exoplanets 62, 74, **74**, 88, **88**, 98, **98**
Extraterrestrials *see* Alien life

F

Fermi paradox 4
Fish in space 176, **176**
Food in space
applesauce 188, **188**
astronaut ice cream 17, **17**
bone-strengthening 92, **92**
chocolate chip cookies 107, **107**
M&M candy 104, **104**
pizza 16, **16**
salt shakers forbidden 86, **86**
sandwiches 102, **102**, 156, **156**
sports drinks **8–9**, 9
sweat and urine as 102, **102**
Fruit flies in space 126, **126**
Full moon 24, **24**, 28, **28**

G

Gagarin, Yuri 25
Gaia spacecraft 190
Galaxies 68, **68**, 79, **79**, 112, 118, **118**, 138, **138**; *see also* Milky Way
Gamma rays 197
Ganymede (Jupiter's moon) 93, **93**
Gemini 3 mission 156
Geysers 95, **95**
Ghost Head Nebula 97, **97**
Glass rain 74
Godzilla (constellation) 197
Goldilocks Zone 194, **194**
Golf balls 131, **131**
Gravity 112, 134, **134**, 139, **139**, 161, **161**
Grogu plush toy 120, **120**
Guatemala 80, **80**

H

Halloween 155, **155**
Haumea (dwarf planet) 151, **151**
Hollow moon theory 16
Hotels 29, **29**, 191, **191**
Houses, UFO-shaped 36, **36–37**
Hubble Space Telescope 41, **41**, **135**, 135–136

Hulk (constellation) 197

I

Iapetus (Saturn's moon) 60, **60**
Ice cream 17, **17**
Ice Worm (robot) 96, **96**
Icy planets 96, **96**
India **14–15**, 15
Insectlike robots 83, **83**
International Space Station (ISS)
  bacteria 56, **56**
  electrical systems 159
  photos of Earth from 170, **170**
  pizza delivery 16, **16**
  recycled sweat and urine 102,
    102
  size 128–129, **128–129**
  slime 30, 134, **134**
  speed 160, **160**
  toilet cost 127
Io (Jupiter's moon) 4, **4**, 84, **84**,
  111, **111**
Ireland 60

J

James Webb Space Telescope
  148–149, 149
Jellyfish in space 126, **126**
"Jingle Bells" (song) 110
Juno spacecraft 144

Jupiter (planet)
  day length 58, **58**
  eating other planets 187, **187**
  green lightning 144, **144**
  moons 4, **4**, 84, **84**, 93, **93**,
    111, **111**
  size **48–49**, 49
  year length 100, **100–101**

L

Lava 114–115, 168, **168**
Lego bricks **166–167**, 167
Lettuce 92, **92**
Life *see* Alien life
Litter boxes 75, **75**
Lunar eclipses 57, **57**
Lunar module 174, **174**

M

Magnetosphere 52
Maha Kumbh Mela **14–15**, 15
M&M candy 104, **104**
Mars (planet)
  day length 59, **59**
  dust tornadoes 146
  evolution 80, **80**
  first helicopter on 123, **123**
  Mariner Valley 98, **98**
  robotic snakes 61, **61**
  rocks falling to Earth 176, **176**

  search for life on 117, **117**
  snowstorms **152–153**, 153
  sounds 12, **12**, 188, **188**
  sunsets **76–77**, 77
  surface 71, **71**
  travel to 27, **27**, 182
  volcanoes 163, **163**
  Wright brothers' plane 123,
    123
  year length 100, **100**
Maya cities 80, **80**
McCandless, Bruce, II 143, **143**
McMinnville, Oregon, U.S.A.
  64–65, **64–65**
Medieval Europe 34, **34**
Mercury (planet) 59, **59**, 100,
  100, 178, **178–179**
Meteorites 8, **8**, 22, **22**, 186, **186**
Meteors 53, 121
Microgravity 93
Middle Ages 34, **34**
Milky Way
  collision 169, **169**
  fiery tsunamis 190, **190**
  hole in 145, **145**
  name 139, **139**
  number of stars born 136
  O-stars 171, **171**
  sandwiched between gas
    bubbles 180, **180**

star map 116

supermassive black hole 94, 168, **168**

time needed to cross 48

Millennium Falcon **184–185,** 185

Mimas (Saturn's moon) 105, **105**

Moon (Earth's moon)

affecting sleep 90, **90**

ancient beliefs 21, 23, **23,** 24, **24,** 28, 34, 92

astronauts on 131, **131,** 140, 174, **174**

blood moon 57, **57**

camps and settlements 24, 54–55, **54–55,** 123

drink powder sent to **8–9,** 9

formation 42–43, **42–43**

full moon 24, **24,** 28, **28**

hollow moon theory 16

lava tubes 114–115

moondust 9, 31, **31,** 131, **131**

moving away from Earth 150

ownership 41, **41**

ring of fire eclipse 57, **57**

rocks and soil 40, **40,** 112, **112,** 188

Sea of Tranquility 168, **168**

shape 110, **110**

shrinking 99, **99**

total lunar eclipse 57, **57**

travel to 27, **27,** 31, **31**

wolves howling at 35, **35**

Moon milk (healing drink) 66, **66**

"Moon trees" 192, **192**

Moondust 9, 31, **31,** 131, **131**

Moonmilk (face cream) 86, **86**

Moonmoon 30, **30**

Moonstone (gem) 92, **92**

Music 110, 147, **147**

N

Nabta Playa, Egypt 38, **38**

NASA

asteroids as spacecraft 48, **48**

astronaut training 195

Halloween playlist 155, **155**

moon base camp 54–55, **54–55**

new constellations 197

selling moondust 31, **31**

swimsuit design 24

see also specific missions and spacecraft

National Air and Space Museum, Washington, D.C. 188

National Cathedral, Washington, D.C. 40, **40**

Nebulae 70, **70,** 97, **97,** 156, **156**

Neptune (planet) **58–59,** 59, 85, 87, **87,** 101, **101,** 162, **162,** 172, **172**

Neutron stars 18–19

Northern lights 62, **62,** 179, **179**

Nuclear pasta 99

Nyberg, Karen 170, **170**

O

O-stars 171, **171**

Olympus Mons, Mars 163, **163**

P

Pac-Man nebula 70, **70**

Pacific Ocean, spacecraft cemetery 20, **20**

Palm Islands, United Arab Emirates 15, **15**

Parker Solar Probe 183, **183,** 186

Pee (urine) 25, 102, **102,** 123

Penguins 110, **110,** 118, **118**

Perseid meteor shower 53, 186, **186**

Perseverance rover 188, **188**

Phytoplankton 14, **14**

Pizza delivery 16, **16**

Planets

day length 58–59, **58–59**

fitting between Earth and moon 6–7, **6–7**

year length 100–101, **100–101**

Plants, grown in space 145

Plasma flare-ups 5, **5**

Pluto (dwarf planet) 134, 172

Poop 44, 88, **88,** 110, **110,** 190, **190**

Pyramids 14, **14**

Q

"Quasi-moons" 164, **164**

R

Radiation shields 44, 69
Rain 74, 113, **113**, 172, **172**
Ring of fire eclipse 57, **57**
Robots 61, **61**, 83, **83**, 96, **96**
Rocket speed 161, **161**
Rogue planets 74, **74**
Roswell, New Mexico, U.S.A. 10–11, **10–11**
Russian astronauts 25

S

Salt 86, **86**
Satellites 20, **20**, 80, **80**, 116
Saturn (planet)
    clouds 177, **177**
    day length 58, **58–59**
    moons 60, **60**, 94–95, **95**, 105, **105**
    polar storm 126, **126**
    rings 71, **71**, 113, **113**, 165
    year length 101, **101**
Sausage stars 175, **175**
Scorpions 28, **28**
Sea of Tranquility 168, **168**
Seeds, launched into space 192
Shepard, Alan 131

16 Psyche (asteroid) 45
Skin 80
Sleep 90, **90**, 139, **139**
Snakes, robotic 61, **61**
Snoopy 142, **142**
Solar eclipses 60, 69, **69**, 154
Solar storms 52, 179, **179**
Solar system 6–7, **6–7**, 13, **13**, 52, 90, **90**
Space, travel time to 26, **26**
Space dust 145
"Space jellyfish" 122, **122**
Space junk 39, **39**, 189, **189**
Space probes 104
"Space rose" (scent) 25, **25**
Space shuttles 25, **25**, 144
Space suits 3, **3**, 62, **62**, 144, 193, **193**, 198–199, **198–199**
Space telescopes 41, **41**, 135, 135–136, **148–149**, 149
Space walks 62, **62**, 125, **125**, 130, **130**, 143, **143**, 181, **181**
Spacecraft cemetery 20, **20**
SpaceShipOne 104
SpaceX 120, 137, **137**
Sports drinks **8–9**, 9
Star Wars (movie series) 72, 105, **105**, 108, **108–109**, 120, **120**, **184–185**, 185
Stardust capsule 193

Stars
    black holes and 46–47, **46–47**
    "blue blobs" 173, **173**
    born in Milky Way 136
    colors 79, 81, **81**
    composition 79
    dead stars 46, **46**, 99
    exploding 138, 156, **156**
    fastest 168, **168**
    fiery tsunamis 190, **190**
    Ghost Head Nebula 97, **97**
    neutron stars 18–19
    O-stars 171, **171**
    Pac-Man nebula 70, **70**
    sausage stars 175, **175**
    star nurseries 32, **32–33**
    teardrop shaped 192
    twinkling 73, **73**
    "vampire star" 132, **132**
    "zombie star" 133
Submarines 94, **94**
Sullivan, Kathryn 130, **130**
Sun
    balls of heat and light 171
    energy needed to reach 182
    fireballs 66, **66**
    medieval beliefs about 34
    noise 124
    Parker Solar Probe 183, **183**, 186

plasma 5, **5**
ring of fire eclipse 57, **57**
size compared to Earth's 21, 28
solar eclipses 60, 69, **69**, 154
solar storms 52, 179, **179**
two suns 13, **13**
Sunsets **76–77**, 77, 122, **122**
Supernova 145
Sweat, recycled 102, **102**
Swimsuits 24
Syzygy 175

T

Tadpole galaxy 138, **138**
Tadpoles in space 176, **176**
Tatooine planets 108, **108–109**
Telescopes
    data turned into sound 138, **138**
    Hubble Space Telescope 41, **41**, **135**, 135–136
    James Webb Space Telescope **148–149**, 149
    percent of universe seen with 182, **182**
    Very Large Telescope 60, **60**
Tesla Roadster car 137, **137**
Tetris 143, **143**
Time travel 50–51, **50–51**

Titan (Saturn's moon) 94
Toothbrush 127, **127**
Top Gun (movie) 151, **151**
Toy Story (movie series) 140, **140–141**

U

UFOs
    cat litter box shaped like 75, **75**
    cover-up of sighting 85, **85**
    festivals 64–65, **64–65**
    first sighting in North America 91, **91**
    hotels shaped like 29, **29**
    houses shaped like 36, **36–37**
    landing pad 24, **24**
    Roswell, New Mexico, U.S.A. 10–11, **10–11**
    see also Alien life
Universe 4, 8, 35, 136
Uranus (planet) 9, **9**, 59, **59**, 101, **101**, 116, **116**, 172, **172**
Urine 25, 102, **102**, 123

V

"Vampire star" 132, **132**
Veil Nebula 156, **156**
Venus (planet) 59, **59**, 100, **100**, 106, **106**, 172

Very Large Telescope 60, **60**
Video games 143, **143**
Volcanoes
    Io 4, **4**, 84, **84**, 111, **111**
    Mars 163, **163**
    moon's lava tubes 114–115
    Pluto 134
    Venus 106, **106**

W

Walt Disney World 67, **67**, 119, **119**
Water clouds 72, **72**
White holes 51
Wolves 35, **35**
World Series 160
Worms in space 93, **93**
Wright brothers 123, **123**

Y

Year length 100–101, **100–101**
Young, John 156

Z

"Zombie star" 133

Since 1888, the National Geographic Society has funded more than 14,000 research, conservation, education, and storytelling projects around the world. National Geographic Partners distributes a portion of the funds it receives from your purchase to National Geographic Society to support programs including the conservation of animals and their habitats. To learn more, visit natgeo.com/info.

For more information, visit nationalgeographic.com, call 1-877-873-6846, or write to the following address:

National Geographic Partners, LLC
1145 17th Street NW
Washington, DC 20036-4688 U.S.A.

More for kids from National Geographic:
natgeokids.com

National Geographic Kids magazine inspires children to explore their world with fun yet educational articles on animals, science, nature, and more. Using fresh storytelling and amazing photography, *Nat Geo Kids* shows kids ages 6 to 14 the fascinating truth about the world—and why they should care. natgeo.com/subscribe

For rights or permissions inquiries, please contact National Geographic Books Subsidiary Rights: bookrights@natgeo.com

Designed by Kathryn Robbins

The publisher would like to thank Paige Towler and Grace Hill, writers; Michelle Harris, fact-checker; Kathryn Williams, project editor; Colin Wheeler, photo editor; Lori Epstein, photo manager; Alix Inchausti, senior production editor; Yogi Carroll and Lisa Walker, production managers; and Lauren Sciortino, associate designer.

Trade paperback ISBN: 978-1-4263-7451-7
Reinforced library binding ISBN: 978-1-4263-7476-0

Printed in China
24/LPC/1

PHOTO CREDITS

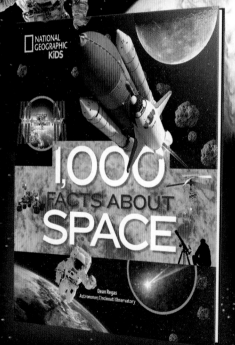